FastTrack
MUSIC INSTRUCTION

For C Diatonic Harmonica

Harmonica 1

W9-BRU-578

INTRODUCTION

You bought a harmonica...so now what?

Congratulations! You look great holding that new harmonica (even as you drive your friends and family crazy with it). But won't your friends and family be impressed when you really learn to play the darn thing?

In just a few weeks, we'll have you playing some very well-known tunes, as well as jamming with some cool riffs and techniques. By the end of this book, you'll be ready to play with a band and play the hits.

All we ask is that you observe the three Ps: **patience**, **practice**, and **pace yourself**.

Don't try to bite off more than you can chew, and DON'T skip ahead. If your lips hurt, take the day off. If you get frustrated, put it down and come back later. If you forget something, go back and learn it again. If you're having a great time, forget about dinner and keep on playing. Most importantly, have fun!

ABOUT THE AUDIO

We're glad you noticed the added bonus—audio tracks! Each music example in the book is included, so you can hear how it sounds and play along when you're ready. Take a listen whenever you see this symbol: ◀1

Each audio example is preceded by one measure of "clicks" to indicate the tempo and meter. Pan right to hear the harmonica part only. Pan left to hear the accompaniment only. As you become more confident, try playing the harmonica part along with the rest of the band.

To access audio visit:
www.halleonard.com/mylibrary
Enter Code
3752-4344-7230-9474

HAL•LEONARD®
CORPORATION
7777 W. BLUEMOUND RD. P.O. BOX 13819 MILWAUKEE, WI 53213

A GOOD PLACE TO START

Your harp is your friend

An instrument can be like a good friend over the years—get you through the rough times and help you sing away the blues. So, before we get started, give your harmonica (or "harp," as it's also called) a name. May we suggest "Harpo?"

Did you buy the right book?

This book teaches you how to play the **diatonic harmonica**, or **C harmonica**. If you have a **chromatic harmonica**, we'll cover that in **FastTrack™ Harmonica 2**. To know whether you have the right kind of harp, check out the two pictures below. You want the one on top. (If you have both, then you are super cool.)

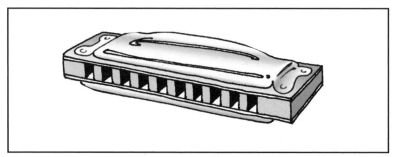

diatonic C harmonica

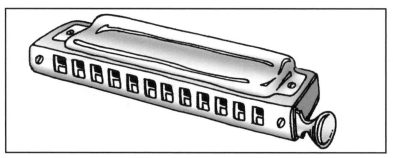

chromatic harmonica

☞ **NOTE:** There are also other diatonic harmonicas (for example, an F diatonic harmonica), so make sure yours is in C for this book. The key of your harp should be stamped on the top cover.

Keep it clean

Fortunately, you've chosen an instrument that doesn't require much maintenance. You won't need any special cleaners or brushes or an annual tuning, but you do need to keep your harmonica clean and dry.

Remember that you'll be playing this thing by blowing air through your mouth. From time to time, there's bound to be some moisture (scientifically called "spit") that collects inside. No problem—just tap it on your palm or pants leg every once in a while. (Try to avoid playing underwater, too!)

And never, we repeat NEVER, play with food in your mouth. First of all, that's pretty gross. Secondly, if you get food in your harmonica, it ain't coming out easily. You don't want to have a smelly or (eventually) insect-filled instrument in your mouth, do you? Well, do you?

Holding the harp

How you hold your harmonica is very important. The best way to hold it is called the **C method**, named after the shape your left hand is in. (We also like to call this the "sock puppet position," for obvious-looking reasons...)

Look at the picture below and follow these steps:

1 Make a "C" with your left hand.

2 Insert the harmonica as shown, holding it firmly but comfortably.

3 Keep your fingers arched slightly. This will allow you to control the sound better.

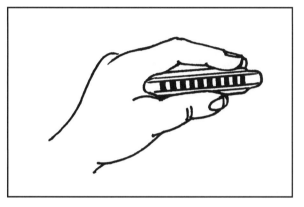

Your right hand should cup, or cradle, your left hand with the fingers coming up around your left hand pinky to form a seal.

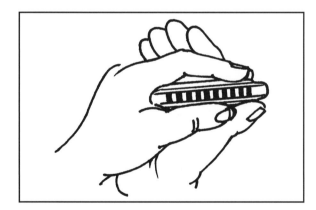

 VERY IMPORTANT: Don't forget to allow room to (a) read the numbers on top and (b) put your lips on the instrument. (Hey, you can't play the harmonica with just your hands, can you?)

By the way, if you're left-handed, read this page again, but reverse the hands. That is, when we say "left hand" use your right hand, and vice versa. Got it?

A FEW MORE THINGS

(...before we jam!)

How your harmonica works

Would you like to know just how that little instrument makes so much sound? Here's how it works...

Unlike the electric guitar or keyboard, the harmonica has no electronics, circuit boards, or other complicated machinery inside. In fact, it's a very simple little music maker, made up of **holes** and **reeds**, sandwiched between two metal plates.

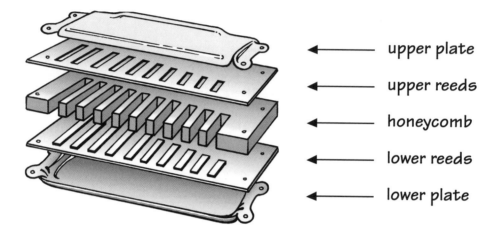

upper plate

upper reeds

honeycomb

lower reeds

lower plate

Inside each hole are two brass reeds, one on top and one on bottom. Each reed is tuned to a different musical pitch. When you **blow** air through a hole, the bottom reed vibrates; when you **draw** (or suck) air through a hole, the top reed vibrates. That's how one hole can produce two separate musical tones.

Go ahead, try it...

Note diagrams

Throughout this book, you will see square box diagrams that look like the one below. This tells you which part of the harmonica will be used for those songs, as well as which notes the holes represent. But before we begin (and for your sheer delight and amusement), listen to all the notes on your C harmonica.

1

Blow	C	E	G	C	E	G	C	E	G	C
Hole	1	2	3	4	5	6	7	8	9	10
Draw	D	G	B	D	F	A	B	D	F	A

☞ If you are comparing this chart to your instrument and find more holes on yours, then (again) you probably have a chromatic harmonica.
Two options: buy **FastTrack™ Harmonica 2** or buy a C harmonica.

4

Please don't swallow it!

You may think that you just put the harp to your mouth and blow. Well, it's not that simple. The position of your mouth and lips on the instrument are important in achieving a good, focused sound.

Don't be timid or germ-conscious about lipping your harmonica (you're the only one playing it). Your lips should be fully around it, almost like you're eating it. In fact, your upper lip should cover half of the top while your lower lip is well beneath. (See the picture below.) You want the inner, wet part of your lips in contact with the harmonica.

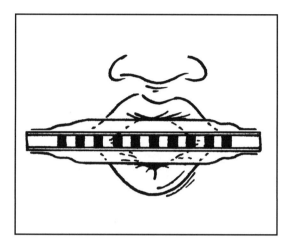 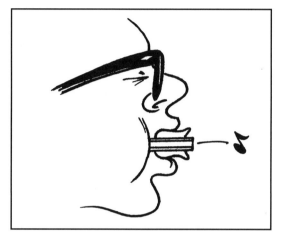

Go ahead and blow a few sounds. Now try drawing (or inhaling) a few. Don't worry about which notes you hear. Right now, you just want to concentrate on how and where it sits in your mouth.

The legend continues...

In addition to the notes and lyrics, you'll find a few more helpful notations in this book's musical examples. These tell you how to play the note. They'll all be clear to you as you continue through the book. For now, just know what they mean by reviewing this legend:

1 – 10	means	**Which hole to play**
↑	means	**Blow (exhale)**
↓	means	**Draw (inhale)**
↗	means	**Half-step blow bend**
↘	means	**Half-step draw bend**

fold

DOG-EAR THESE TWO PAGES
(...you'll need to review them later)

Music is a language with its own symbols, structure, and rules (and exceptions to those rules). To read, write, and play music requires knowing all the symbols and rules. But let's take it one step at a time (a few now, a few later as we go along)...

Notes

Music is written with little doo-hickeys called **notes.** Notes come in all shapes and sizes. A note has two essential characteristics: **pitch** (indicated by its position on the staff) and **rhythmic value** (indicated by the following symbols):

whole note	half note	quarter note
(four beats)	(two beats)	(one beat)

The rhythmic value lets you know how many beats the note lasts. Most commonly, a quarter note equals one beat. After that it's just like fractions (we hate math, too!):

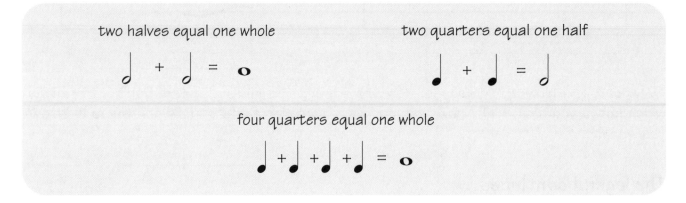

Staff

All the notes are positioned on (or nearby) a **staff,** which consists of five parallel lines and four spaces. (The plural for staff is "staves.") Each line and space represents a different pitch.

Ledger Lines

Since not all notes will fit on just five lines and four spaces, **ledger lines** are used to extend the staff:

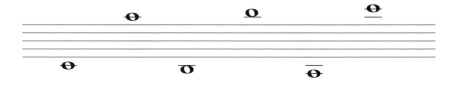

Clef

A symbol called a **clef** indicates which pitches appear on a particular staff. Music uses a variety of clefs, but we're only concerned with one for now:

treble clef →

A **treble clef** makes the staff lines and spaces have the following pitches:

E	G	B	D	F
Every	Good	Band	Draws	Fans

F A C E
"FACE"

An easy way to remember the line pitches is "**E**very **G**ood **B**and **D**raws **F**ans." For the spaces, spell "**face**."

Measures (or Bars)

Notes on a staff are divided into **measures** (or "bars") to help you keep track of where you are in the song. (Imagine reading a book without any periods, commas, or capital letters!)

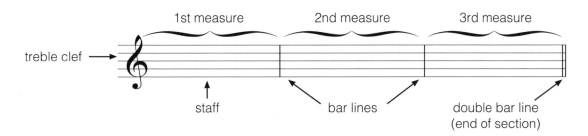

1st measure   2nd measure   3rd measure

treble clef →

staff   bar lines   double bar line
(end of section)

Time Signatures (or Meters)

A **time signature** (or "meter") indicates how many beats will appear in each measure. It contains two numbers: the top number tells you how many beats will be in each measure; the bottom number says what type of note will equal one beat.

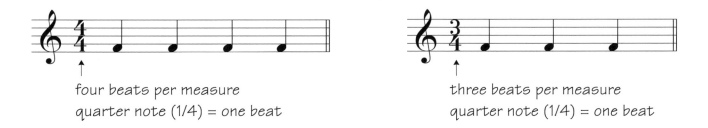

four beats per measure
quarter note (1/4) = one beat

three beats per measure
quarter note (1/4) = one beat

☞   **R**elax for a while, read through it again later, and then move on.
(Trust us—as we go through the book, you'll start to understand it.)

LESSON 1

Don't just sit there, play something!

If you've already tried playing your harmonica, chances are you've heard several different notes at once. That's because you're blowing or drawing air through more than one hole at a time. With practice, you can learn to direct air through a single hole.

Pucker up and blow!

Playing one, two, or three notes is determined by the shape of your lips. To play single notes, we use the **pucker method**. With the harp still well within your mouth (see below), tighten and pucker your lips like you are going to whistle a happy tune, or drink from a straw.

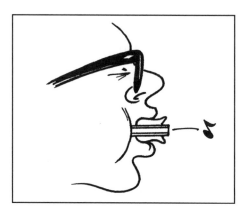 

When you pucker, you can direct air through one single hole at a time. When you relax your lips (or "unpucker," if that's even a word), you can play two or three notes. Let's try it...

Put your mouth around Holes 4 to 6 and **blow**. You should hear the notes of all three holes (C, E, G). Now pucker, directing air through the middle hole (Hole 5) and making a single note (E). Do this several times with the following example:

6		6		6		6
5	5	5		5	5	5
4		4		4		4
↑	↑	↑		↑	↑	↑

Hey, it sounds like the start of "This Old Man." Wow, your first song!

Same idea in reverse...

Now let's try the same thing, but this time you'll **draw** (or inhale). When you do this, of course, you hear slightly different notes than before—those on the top reed actually. With unpuckered lips, you get three notes (D, F, A); puckered, you should hear just one (F):

6		6		6		6
5	5	5		5	5	5
4		4		4		4
↓	↓	↓		↓	↓	↓

It's OK to cheat...for now

If you're having trouble playing single notes, or even finding the right holes to put your mouth around, try this trick:

To find and play Hole 5, for example, cover Holes 1 to 4 with your left index finger and Holes 6 to 10 with your right. (See the illustration below.) Now put the entire finger-harp apparatus to your mouth and blow or draw Hole 5.

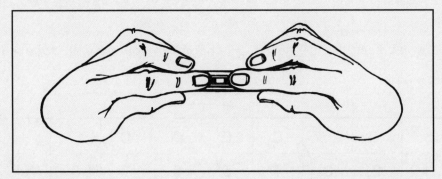

Because it's so darn awkward, we're convinced we don't need to tell you that this is not a correct (or even realistic) way to play the harp. (Oops! Too late—we already did.) But it is a great way to figure out what pitch you're supposed to be playing, if you're having trouble finding it.

Breathing is important!

With all this inhaling and exhaling, you'd think breathing would be no problem while playing the harmonica. Au contraire, mon frere! It's very important to stay aware of when and how you breathe while you play.

To take a quick breath between notes, move the harmonica slightly away from your lower lip while using your upper lip to keep your position. It's not as difficult as it sounds, but it's not as easy as you'd think either. Try it with the next song...

◆4 5↑   5↓   5↑ ,   5↑   5↓   5↑ ,   5↑   5↑   5↑

5↑   5↓   5↑ ,   6/5/4↑   6/5/4↓   6/5/4↑ ,   6/5/4↑   6/5/4↓   6/5/4↑

Of course, if you're consistently alternating between blowing and drawing, you may not need to take a breath. But this technique will come in handy sometimes.

WHAT'S THAT?
The "," symbol is a breath mark.
Take a quick but deep breath whenever you see it.

Your C diatonic harmonica is in the **key of C**. This simply means that it uses the following musical notes:

C — D — E — F — G — A — B — C

"But wait!" you say. "That's only eight notes, and my harmonica has ten holes!" Correct, Einstein—most of these notes repeat several times so that you can play the same notes higher or lower.

But for now you won't need twenty notes. All the notes you need are located in the middle, on Holes 4 to 7.

Blow				C	E	G	C			
Hole	1	2	3	4	5	6	7	8	9	10
Draw				D	F	A	B			

Playing in the middle section of the harmonica is called **straight harp** because you are using the notes best suited for your instrument. Using the pucker method, try blowing and drawing through Holes 4 through 7, one at a time. (Use the notation below as a guide.)

◆ 5 From C to Shining C

C	D	E	F	G	A	B	C
4↑	4↓	5↑	5↓	6↑	6↓	7↓	7↑

Congratulations! (Sure, it needs lots of practice, but that was your first try!) Try again until you're pleased with the sound of the notes and comfortable with moving your lips back and forth between the four holes.

Don't worry too much if you aren't getting a true single-note sound.
If the sound of surrounding holes is "leaking" a bit as you play—no big deal!
Concentrate on centering your pucker around the correct hole.
It'll still sound great, and with practice, it'll fix itself.

Now try a real song, reading from the same type of harmonica notation as before. Remember, though, that this is not real music notation, and you won't often see this in music (except for beginning harmonica books). So don't get too attached to it.

COUNT THIS: The little numbers under the lyrics are the **beats**. Count them in your head as you play, to know how long a note should be held.

◆6 Brother Jacques Rock

4↑	4↓	5↑	4↑ﾞ	4↑	4↓	5↑	4↑ﾞ
Are	you	sleep -	ing,	are	you	sleep -	ing,
count: 1	2	3	4	1	2	3	4

5↑	5↓	6↑	ﾞ	5↑	5↓	6↑	ﾞ
Broth -	er	Jacques,		Broth -	er	Jacques?	
1	2	3	(4)	1	2	3	(4)

6↑	5↓	5↑	4↑ﾞ	6↑	5↓	5↑	4↑ﾞ
Crowds	are	wait -	ing,	crowds	are	wait -	ing,
1	2	3	4	1	2	3	4

4↑	4↓	4↑	ﾞ	4↑	4↓	4↑	
Check	the	clock.		Time	to	rock.	
1	2	3	(4)	1	2	3	(4)

This next song starts on Hole 5 (E). Listen to the audio if you need a reference for how it should sound.

◆7 Ode to Joyful Rock

5↑	5↑	5↓	6↑	6↑	5↓	5↑	4↓
count: 1	2	3	4	1	2	3	4

4↑	4↑	4↓	5↑	5↑		4↓	ﾞ
1	2	3	4	1	(2)	3	(4)

5↑	5↑	5↓	6↑	6↑	5↓	5↑	4↓
1	2	3	4	1	2	3	4

4↑	4↑	4↓	5↑	4↓		4↑	
1	2	3	4	1	(2)	3	(4)

Before moving on, we suggest playing through this lesson again.
Make sure you know how to read the number/arrow notation before we learn real notation.

LESSON 2

Get out your staff and clef...

Unless you intend to play all your music from a beginning harmonica book (boring!), you won't often encounter the "number/arrow" harmonica notation we used in Lesson 1. Most of life's music is printed in standard music notation. So, before proceeding, flip back to pages 6 and 7 for a review. (We'll wait...)

Notes: C, D, E, F, G, A

Let's take this reading music thing gradually, a few notes at a time. We'll start with six easy notes found on Holes 4 through 6.

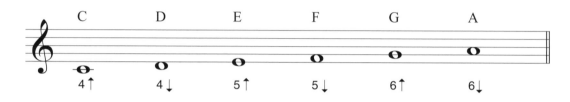

Now that you know what they look like, here's a song to test them out. Don't forget to pucker...

☞ IMPORTANT: Just like reading a book, when you get to the end of the musical line (staff), continue on to the beginning of the next line. The song is over when you see the double (thin and thick) barline.

⑧ Mary Had a Little Band

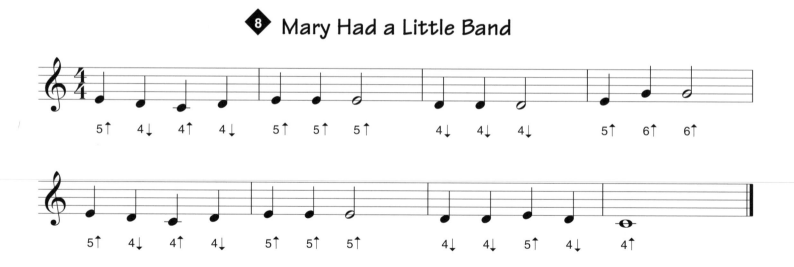

Notice that as the notes go down the staff, your mouth goes down the harp. Likewise, as the notes go up the staff, your mouth goes...oh, you get the idea! Try it again—this time with the audio.

Tonguing

When playing repeated notes (like in measure 2 of the last song), it's important to clearly define the beginning and ending of each note. Otherwise, you'll get a muddy, sloppy sound. This type of definition is called **articulation**, an important technique for any harmonica player.

One way to achieve good articulation is with your tongue. Try this little exercise **without** your harmonica:

 1 Say "ta" four times slowly. Notice where your tongue touches the roof of your mouth.

2 Now say "ta" but hold it— "taaaaaaaaaaaaaaaaaaa."

3 Say it loud; whisper it.

Now do the exact same thing while blowing a single note on the harmonica. Each time your tongue touches the roof of your mouth, it cuts off the air flow through your harmonica (even though very briefly), which gives a definite start and stop to each note.

◆ 9 Ta-Ta for Now

> HELPFUL HINT: Experiment with other tonguing sounds like "da" and "ka."
> Try a fast tonguing with "ta-da, ta-da, ta-da" as you continue
> to blow steadily. (Or if you're hungry, use "taco, taco.")

Continue practicing your tonguing technique with this well-known song:

◆ 10 Twinkle, Twinkle, Little Rock Star

A FINE TIME TO BREATHE

Up to now, you've been using those handy little breath marks as signals to breathe and avoid fainting. Well, not always will the music be so kind as to remind you. So, you have to find other places to breathe. Have we got a perfect solution for you...

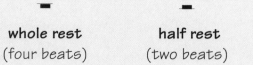

Rests

A musical **rest** is a pause, some short and some long. Rests are like notes in that they have their own rhythmic values, instructing the musician how long (or how many beats) to pause:

—	—	ξ
whole rest	**half rest**	**quarter rest**
(four beats)	(two beats)	(one beat)

Use these new squigglies to your advantage. Whenever you see one, take a deep breath while counting the beat in your head.

In the following 4/4 example, you will blow on hole 6 like this: G, G, pause, G, pause, pause, pause, pause, G, G, pause, pause, G, pause, pause, G.

⓫ Take a Load Off

IMPORTANT: A rest does not mean rest your hands or put your harmonica down! During a rest, you should take a deep breath and get your mouth into position for the next set of notes.

⓬ This Old Man

14

Make sure you plan ahead!

Before you start playing a song, take a look and see which parts might be problematic for breathing. For example, in the next song, you will play six exhaled notes in a row (starting at measure 10) without a chance to breathe—that is, no rests. This means you should take a very deep breath on the rest just before this part, so you might want to circle it or something.

⑬ When the Saints Go Marching In

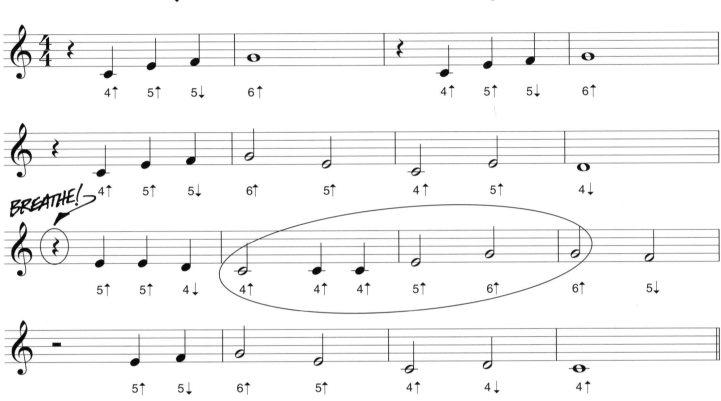

Nice tie!

And you thought you were running out of breath with whole notes? Take a deep breath, because you're about to encounter even longer notes...

A **tie** connects two notes (makes 'em look fancy) and tells you to extend the first note (keep playing) through to the end of the tied note:

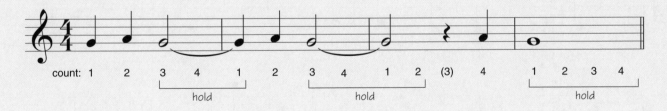

Turn the page and try playing a song with some sharp-dressed (tied) notes...

Remember to think and count the beat in your head as you hold a note. After a while, this will become second nature—you'll just feel the beat.

◆14 Kum-bah-yah

4↑ 5↑ 6↑ 6↑ 6↑   6↓ 6↓ 6↑   4↑ 5↑

6↑ 6↑ 6↑   5↓ 5↑ 4↓   4↑ 5↑ 6↑ 6↑ 6↑   6↓ 6↓

6↑   5↓   5↑ 4↑   4↓ 4↓ 4↑

Further extensions

Another way to extend the rhythmic value of a note is to use a **dot**. A dot extends the note by one-half of the note's original value. Most common is the dotted half note:

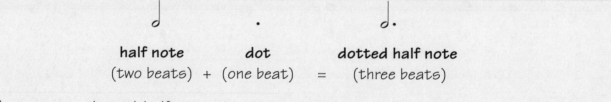

half note   **dot**   **dotted half note**
(two beats)   +   (one beat)   =   (three beats)

You'll encounter dotted half notes in many songs, especially those that use 3/4 meter (that is, three beats per measure).

◆15 Harp Waltz

4↑ 4↓ 4↓ 4↑ 4↑ 5↑ 5↑   4↑ 4↓ 4↓   4↑

5↑ 5↓ 6↑   5↑ 4↓ 4↑   4↓   5↑   4↑

◆ 16 Camptown Races

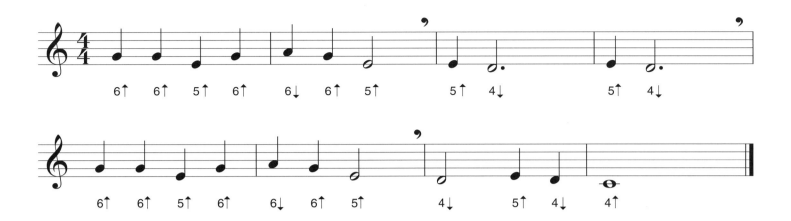

Pickups aren't just trucks...

By the way, instead of starting a song with rests (like "Kum-bah-ya,") a **pickup measure** can be used. A pickup measure simply deletes the rests at the beginning. So, if a pickup has only one beat, you count "1, 2, 3" and start playing on beat 4:

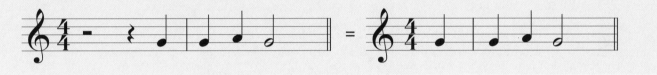

Try this song with a pickup measure. Listen to Track 17 to get an idea of how it starts. Count "1, 2, 3, 1, 2," and then play away.

◆ 17 For He's a Jolly Good Fellow

This is a good time to take a break, maybe order a pizza.
When you come back, gargle some mouthwash
and play the songs in Lessons 1 and 2 again.

LESSON 3
Movin' on up...

Reading six different notes (C to A) in musical notation wasn't too difficult, was it? Great! Let's add two more higher notes...

Notes: B and C

For the other six notes (C through A), you played them consecutively—alternating blows and draws—as you went up the staff. When you reach Hole 7, your inclination is to (again) blow the lower note (B) and draw the higher one (C).

But wait: These new notes are tricky! B and C are reversed on Hole 7. You draw the lower (B) and blow the higher (C). To play all eight notes in order, you follow this pattern:

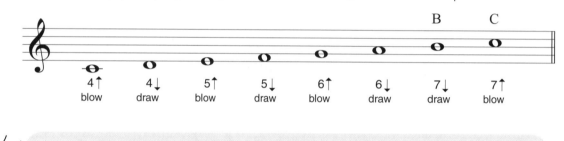

LEARN SOMETHING NEW! Do you realize what you just played?
That was your first musical **scale**!

Great, but what's a scale?

A scale is nothing more than an arrangement of notes in specific patterns of "half steps" and "whole steps." Using a piano diagram to illustrate, a **half step** is from one key to the next closest key (black or white); two keys apart is a **whole step**.

The notes on your harmonica are equivalent to the white keys on a piano. The black keys have other names like C-sharp and B-flat, which you'll encounter later when you learn to **bend** notes. (Much later, pal.)

But just because you have the white-key notes doesn't mean that you don't have half steps. Look at the distance between E and F or B and C above. (Yep—half step.)

The step pattern used for a major scale is:

Whole — Whole — Half — Whole — Whole — Whole — Half

Most scales have eight notes and begin and end on the same-named note. The scale you played started (and ended) on C and used the **major pattern** above, thus it was the **C major scale**.

Put it to work!

The next song uses all eight of these notes, starting at the top and working your way down. It's a well-known holiday song, but it's also a backwards C major scale!

◆18 Joy to the World

NOTE: A rest isn't only for inhaling. In "Joy to the World," the notes in measures 5 and 6 were all drawn (inhaled) notes. But if you inhale on the rests, too, you have too much air! In this case, the rests give you a chance to exhale.

To blow or not to blow?

How often are the notes of a song arranged in the same order as a scale—backward or forward? (Let's hope not many. It would get quite boring!) So, remembering the blow/draw pattern of a C scale won't be much help to you.

Instead, playing the harmonica requires memorization. You have to remember which notes are blown and which are drawn…and you have to remember it lightning fast! One way to do this is to think:

1 All Cs, Es, and Gs are **blown**, except for the G on Hole 2.

2 All other notes (D, F, A, B) are **drawn**.

Test your memory with some music. In the first example, you'll be jamming on all the blow notes (that is, Cs, Es, and Gs). Then move on to a short example of the drawn notes—D, F, A, B. (NOTE: Each example is played twice on the track, immediately followed by the next one.)

◆19 Blow and Draw

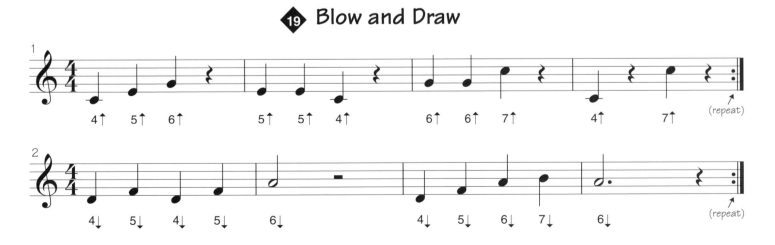

Knowing scales is the key...

If a song's melody is derived from the notes of the C major scale, the song is in the **key of C**. (The scale is your "key" to which notes to play!) Since your C harmonica is based on the notes of the C major scale, your harmonica is in the key of C.

The great thing about a diatonic harmonica is that you really can't play a wrong note. Seriously! Track 20 is a tune in the key of C. All of the notes and harmony in this little ditty come from the C major scale. Listen to it a couple of times...

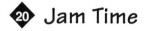 **Jam Time**

Now put your harp to your mouth and jam along with the audio—single or multiple notes. Don't even think about the actual notes you're playing. Nine times out of ten, it will sound pretty darn good. Why? Because you're playing in the same **key** as the tune!

Notes with the most

Of course, you want to sound good ten times out of ten, so you should know which scale notes are the most important, or most often used. It's as easy as counting to five...

In the key of C, the most common notes are the **first**, **third**, and **fifth** notes of the scale:

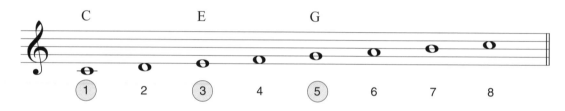

Hey, those are all blow notes! (Told you it was easy.) **C**, **E**, and **G** are the notes used to make a C chord (we'll explain chords in the next lesson), and a C chord is the one used most often when playing a song in the key of C.

Try jamming along with Track 20 again while playing only C, E, and Gs. You can use the little idea shown below, or make up your own.

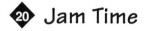 **Jam Time**

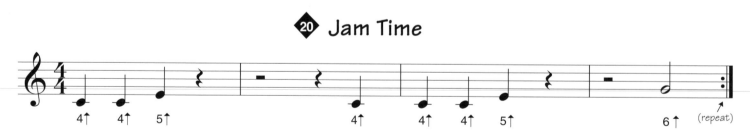

NEW TERM: Short musical ideas like the one shown in Track 20 are called **riffs**.
While the rest of the band is playing the song,
you can insert your riff wherever you think appropriate.

Playing only three notes (C, E, G) can get boring, so you throw a few drawn notes into your riffs to spice things up. Try this using the riffs shown below first, before making up your own...

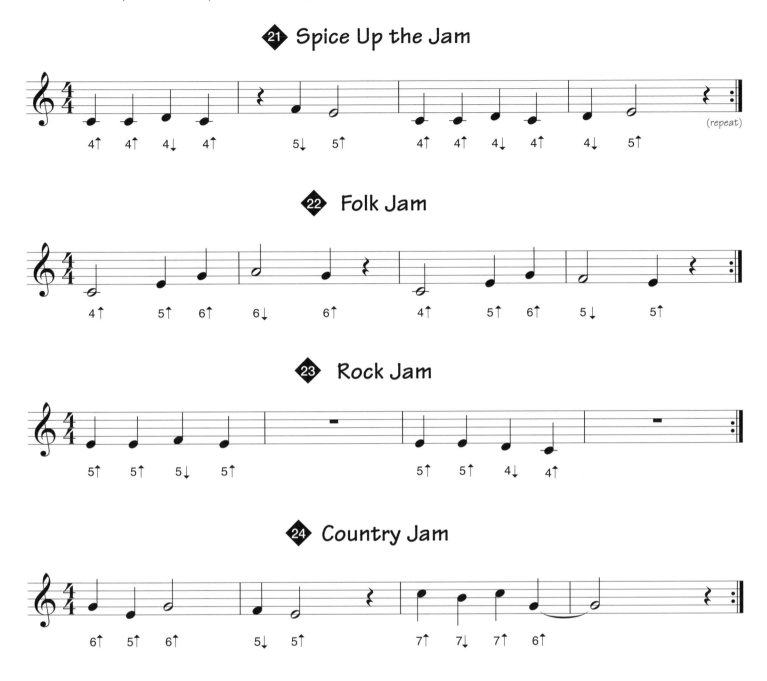

21 Spice Up the Jam

4↑ 4↑ 4↓ 4↑   5↓ 5↑   4↑ 4↑ 4↓ 4↑ 4↓ 5↑

(repeat)

22 Folk Jam

4↑ 5↑ 6↑ 6↓ 6↑   4↑ 5↑ 6↑ 5↓ 5↑

23 Rock Jam

5↑ 5↑ 5↓ 5↑   5↑ 5↑ 4↓ 4↑

24 Country Jam

6↑ 5↑ 6↑   5↓ 5↑   7↑ 7↓ 7↑ 6↑

Each riff comes from notes of the C major scale. The band is playing in the key of C, so it works out no matter where you play the riff. Cool, huh?

COINCIDENCE OR HIDDEN AGENDA?
Diatonic harmonicas are designed so that the most important
notes of the key are blown. This makes it easy to improvise and still sound good.
Since your harp is a **C diatonic** harp,
the blow notes are the three most important (C, E, G).

Get into the zone!

With so many notes (20 to be exact) and possible places to play on the harmonica, it's easy to get confused. So, it helps to break down (not literally, please) your harp into three separate sections. We'll call these **zones**.

	Zone 3			Zone 1			Zone 2			
Blow	C	E	G	C	E	G	C	E	G	C
Hole	1	2	3	4	5	6	7	8	9	10
Draw	D	G	B	D	F	A	B	D	F	A

Zone 1 (middle): Good for playing just about any song in the key of C. Hey, all the notes are there!

Zone 2 (upper): Good for higher notes. You don't have to stop at Hole 7!

Zone 3 (lower): Good for playing lower notes or for playing harmony. (We'll cover this in the next lesson.)

☞ IMPORTANT: You aren't limited to a particular zone. When necessary, you'll need to go outside of the zone you're playing in to grab extra notes.

By now, you probably have the notes of Zone 1 down. Let's try some songs that use higher notes, from Zone 2…

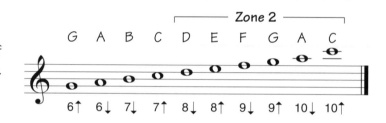

25 Home on the Range

The next song is all in Zone 2, except for the G (Hole 6) that you occassionally drop down to play. And even though it's Zone 2, most of the melody notes are blown (C, E, and G again), since this song is (yep!) in the key of C...

26 ▸ The Streets of Laredo

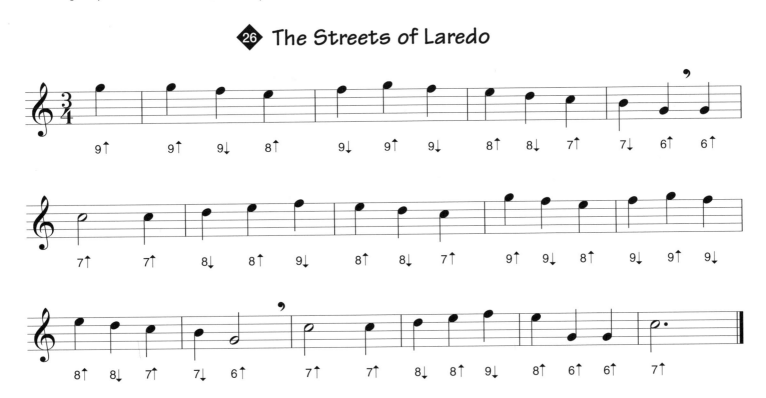

Let's sing this lesson to sleep with an old nighttime classic, "Taps." (Breathe whenever you can, because all the notes are blow notes!)

Taps

27

HAVE SOME FUN!
Say the word "yo" (or even "yo-yo") as you play the songs again.
You'll hear a sorta wobbly, cowboy sound. (Yee-haw!)

LESSON 4
In perfect harmony!

Sometimes you just don't want to play the melody. Maybe you're tired, or maybe the singer in your band is doing fine without you. In these cases, you can play an accompaniment part, or **harmony**. And as we said before, Zone 3 is the perfect place for doing this.

Zone 3: Chords

When you play multiple notes at the same time, you are playing **chords**. Chords supply harmony to a song. Your tiny but highly versatile instrument can play either single melody notes or chords. (Hey, your sax-playing friend can't do that!)

If you don't feel like playing riffs or melodies, you can just play the chords of a song. And without really knowing how to play a harmonica, you can play two basic chords—C and G:

1 Put your mouth on the bottom three holes (1, 2, and 3).

2 Blow, and you will hear C, E, G—a C chord.

3 Draw, and you will hear D, G, B—a G chord.

Try it with a song. Use the letters above the staff (the **chord symbols**) to know which chord to play. Blow for C; draw for G. You can either hold the chord or play a rhythm with it.

◆28 Oh, Susannah

Thank you, sir. May we have another? This time, try to play the correct rhythm with your chords. Listen to the audio to get an idea of what we mean.

◆29 Rock to My Lou

What exactly is a chord?

Most chords contain three scale notes—the **root, third,** and **fifth**—each being a specific number of steps from the other. The chord's name (C or G) comes from the **root** note. The **third** is two scale notes higher than the root, and the **fifth** is two scale notes higher than the third.

Using the C major scale, it's easy to find the notes for a C chord:

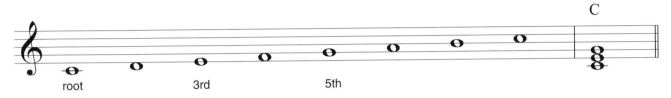

To build a G chord, we can create a G scale and take its root, third, and fifth notes:

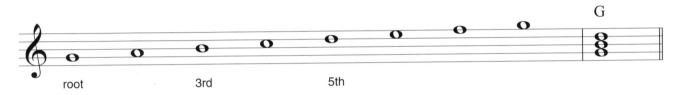

To play these chords, find spots on your harmonica where the three notes of the chord are grouped. For example, notice that no matter where you put your mouth, you will always get the notes of a C chord when you blow:

Blow	C	E	G	C	E	G	C	E	G	C
Hole	1	2	3	4	5	6	7	8	9	10

But to play a G chord (G-B-D), you really only have two choices to draw on:

Hole	1	2	3	4	5	6	7	8	9	10
Draw	D	G	B	D	F	A	B	D	F	A

Not many alternatives for such a popular chord, so we need a solution...

Two-note chords

Technically speaking, a chord has three or more notes. But we can cheat a little and sometimes use only two notes for harmony. You just have to choose which note to drop. This will usually depend on where you want to play the two-note chord.

Look at your G chord. It has the notes G-B-D. If you drop the G and just play B-D, then you have two different places now to play a G chord—one low and one high.

	1	2	3	4	5	6	7	8	9	10
Draw	D	G	B	D	F	A	B	D	F	A

Try all of your G chord possibilities:

30 ◆ More G Chords

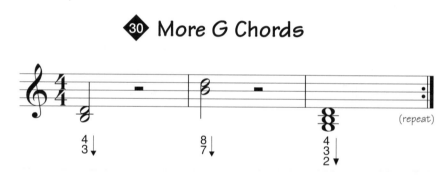

Another very handy chord to know is the F chord, made up of the scale notes F-A-C.

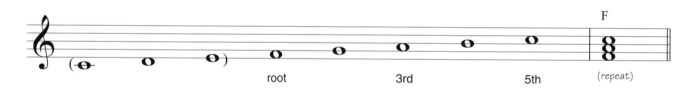

Since two of the notes are drawn (F and A) and one is blown (C), you will absolutely never be able to play F, A, and C at the same time. No problem—drop the C and just play F and A. Now you have two choices, Holes 5-6 or Holes 9-10:

31 ◆ My New F Chord

26

YOU STILL GOT RHYTHM!

Can you spare a quarter? How 'bout an eighth?

An **eighth note** has a flag on it: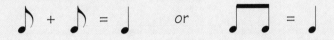

Two eighths equal one quarter note (or one beat). To make it easier on the eyes (you're welcome!), eighth notes are connected with a **beam**:

To count eighth notes, divide the beat into two and use "and" between the beats:

Practice this by first counting out loud while you tap your foot on the beats. The second time, keep your foot tapping the beat while you sing the crazy lyrics "1 and, 2 and," etc.

32

1 (&) 2 (&) 3 & 4 (&)   1 & 2 & 3 (&) 4 (&)

What about the rest?

Eighth rests are the same (value-wise), but you…pause. Count, tap and pause with track 33:

33

1 (&) 2 (&) (3) & 4 (&)   1 & 2 (&) 3 & (4) &

Practice eighth notes while you also practice your new C, F, and G chords. Don't worry too much about how you sound. The main thing is to get this new rhythm down.

34 Chord/Rhythm Jam

That's all you need to know...seriously! C, G, and F are pretty much the only chords you need to play almost any song in the key of C! Sure, you'll learn more in later lessons, but these three are the most common. And here's proof—two solid pages of three-chord songs!

Play from the chord symbols above the staff. Try holding some chords and improvising a rhythm on others. Just have fun...

35 ◆ Amazing Grace

IMPORTANT: Don't forget to articulate as you play each chord. Say "ta" or "da" or "ka" to give each chord a definite beginning and ending.

36 ◆ Rockin' on Old Smokey

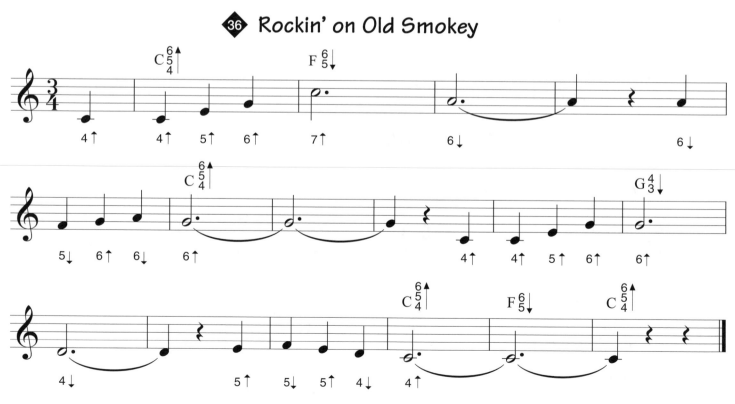

28

37 Yankee Doodle

NOTE: The letters "N.C." stand for no chord. So, don't play anything there. Instead, take a deep breath and get ready to play the next chord.

38 Down in the Valley

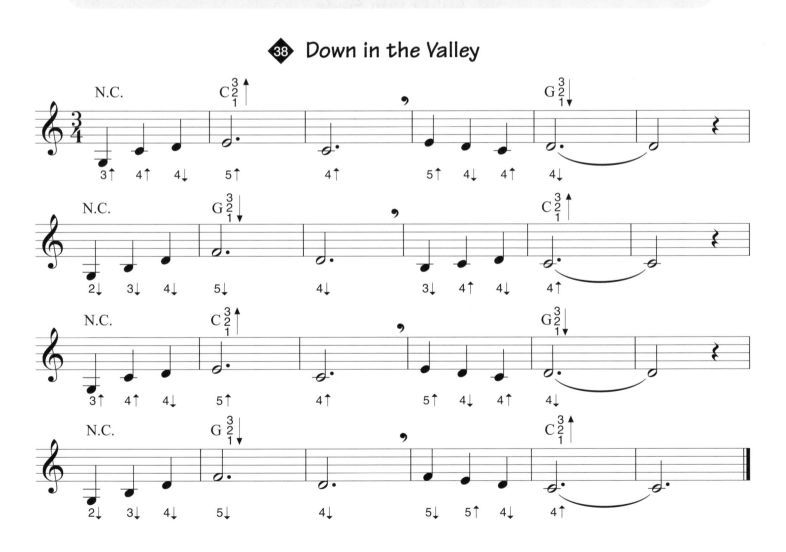

Try playing these two pages again, but this time play the melodies instead of the chords.

Remember the dotted half note (three beats)? A **dotted quarter** note gets one and a half beats:

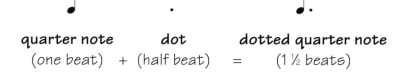

quarter note   **dot**   **dotted quarter note**
(one beat)   +   (half beat)   =   (1 ½ beats)

Think of it as being a quarter note tied to an eighth note.

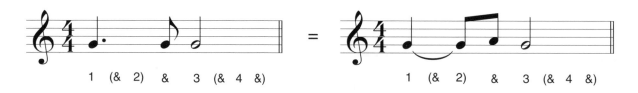

Often you'll see a dotted quarter note paired with an eighth note, since the eighth equals the missing half beat. Listen to Track 39 while you clap the beat. Once you can feel the rhythm of the dotted quarter note, try playing it...

◆39 Auld Lang Syne

WARNING: If you haven't slept since page 1,
continuing could be hazardous to an enjoyable musical life.
Take a long break and go sleep!
(Your neighbors need a break on the ears, too.)

LESSON 5
Playin' the blues

You know chords, scales, all the notes, some different rhythms, lots of good stuff. We think it's time to make your little harp sing a new kind of tune—the **blues**.

Cross harp

Since your harmonica is in the key of C, playing songs in other keys on it is called **cross harp**. Who cares why exactly—it's just a hip little name. Whatever the reason, it's an important concept to know, because there are lots of songs in other keys.

The **key of G** is a popular one. And on the harmonica, it's a great key for playing the blues. If you make a scale on the root note G, you get the following:

40 G Blues

HEAD FOR THE END ZONE: When you play G blues, you'll find yourself using Zone 3 quite a bit. And while you're down there, you can jam those G and C chords some more.

You'll find that many of the notes in cross-harp blues playing are drawn. Keep this consistent by playing the low G on Hole 2 (drawn).

41 Roadkill Blues

ONE POWERFUL NOTE

OK, so you want to know how the blues works. How can the sound be so different from the songs and riffs we played in C? If you recall the steps used to form a major scale, you might remember that the last two steps are **whole step-half step**, as shown on the C major scale below.

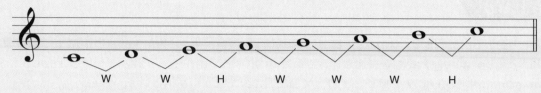

But when you play a scale on the root note G, the last two steps are reversed (**half step-whole step**).

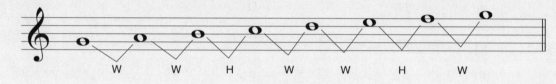

Your ear expects the seventh note (F) to sound a half-step higher. When it doesn't, it makes the whole scale sound kinda "bluesy." That F is one powerful little note, huh?

Feel the power of F as you make your own kind of blues with the following riffs.

42 G Blues Riff

43 Extended Riff

You can use your chords to riff, too.

44 Blues Chords Riff

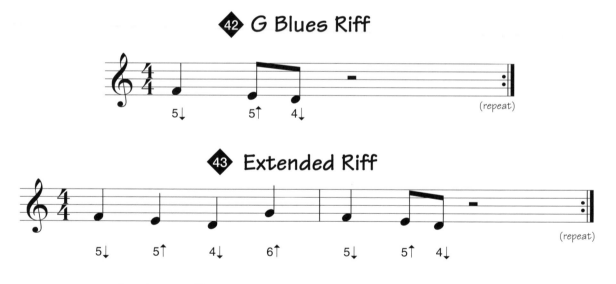

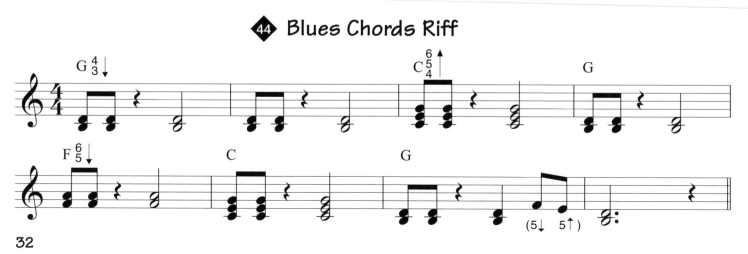

Of course, some songs in G don't even use the omnipotent F, so they don't sound like the blues. They just sound like normal tunes. Try the next two, for example:

45 Red River Valley

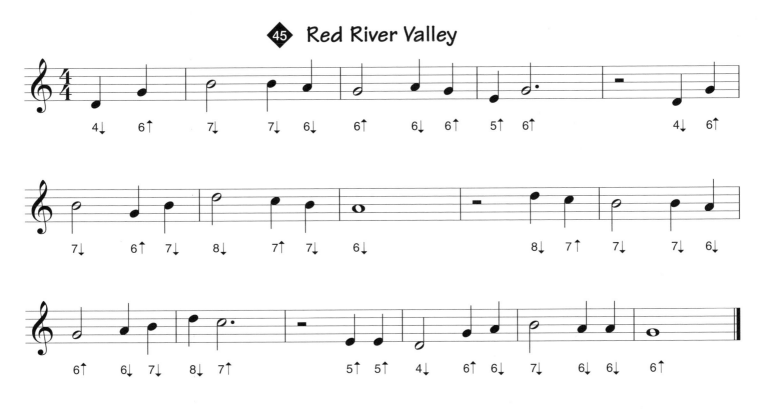

46 Tom Dooley

CAUTION: This next song has a difficult-looking rhythm (eighth-quarter-eighth). It's actually pretty easy, though. Take a listen to Track 46 first to get a feel for it.

WHAT'S THAT SYMBOL?

Repeat signs (‖: :‖) tell you to (you guessed it!) repeat everything in between.
If only one sign appears at the end (:‖), repeat from the beginning of the song.

More notes for your money

Well, we lied (so sue us). Playing the G blues isn't really playing in the **key of G**. Actually, the key of G is based on the **G major scale**, which (like the C major scale) has the following step pattern:

Whole — Whole — Half — Whole — Whole — Whole — Half

If you were playing a piano, notice that this pattern and scale would require you to play a black key—the one between F and G.

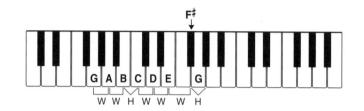

When a song, scale or key requires a note that is a half step higher or lower than the normal-sounding note, a symbol is placed by that note.

One half step higher is called a **sharp** and looks like a tic-tac-toe board:

One half step lower is called a **flat** and looks like a backwards note with no air in it (get it? "flat"):

So, the correct G major scale (which requires F to be a half-step higher, F-sharp) is notated and sounds like this:

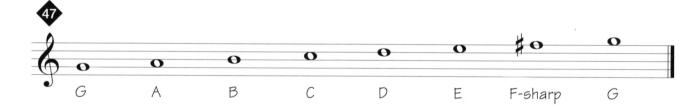

As you know all to well, you don't have any sharp or flat notes. You just have ten holes and twenty notes, right? Right??

Well, not anymore...

To play sharps and flats requires a special technique called **note bending**. You aren't really bending anything or hurting your fragile little instrument. When you "bend" a note on your harmonica, you **lower** the sound of the note.

To bend a note, you apply more pressure to your note-playing than usual. The easiest notes to bend are ones that are drawn on Holes 1 through 4. Follow these steps:

For draw bends:

1 Draw air through the correct hole.

2 At the same time, lower your jaw.

3 Also at the same time, curve your tongue back in a rounded position.

👉 HELPFUL HINT: For draw bends, say "AUHH" as you play. This will put your jaw in the correct position to bend the note.

Try bending some draw notes on your harmonica, starting with the lowest one.

48

Hole	1	2	3	4	5	6	7	8	9	10
Draw	D	G	B	D	F	A	B	D	F	A
Bend	D♭/C#	G♭/F#	B♭/A#	D♭/C#						

Now enjoy some of these new notes in a blues tune:

49 Bendy Blues

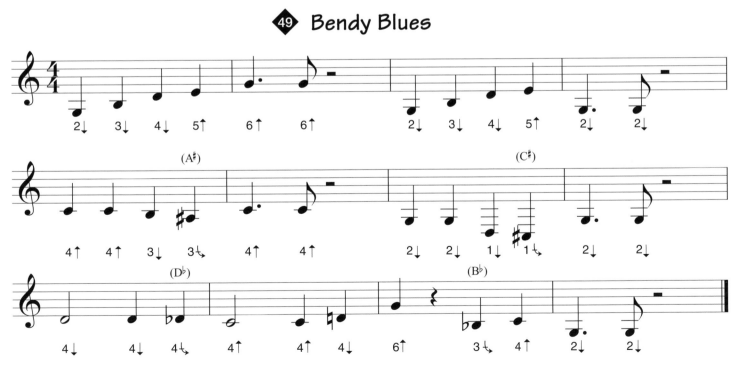

The blow bends are a bit more difficult, but the technique is similar. Keep in mind that it only works well on Holes 8, 9, and 10. Here are the steps:

For blow bends:

 1 Blow air through the correct hole.

2 At the same time, move your jaw back slightly.

3 Also at the same time, curve your tongue back in a rounded position.

👉 HELPFUL HINT: For blow bends, saying "OHH" as you play puts your jaw in the correct position to bend the note.

◆50								Bend	$\frac{E^\flat}{D^\sharp}$	$\frac{G^\flat}{F^\sharp}$	B
Blow	C	E	G	C	E	G	C	E	G	C
Hole	1	2	3	4	5	6	7	8	9	10

Think backwards

If it's not possible to bend a note up (or higher), how can you ever play sharps? Good question.

Look again at the keyboard diagram on page 34. The note between F and G can be called either **F-sharp** or **G-flat**. That's right—every sharp note has a corresponding flat name. Since you can't bend a note higher, you have to think of F-sharp as "lowering" (bending) the note G…

◆51 Worried Man Blues

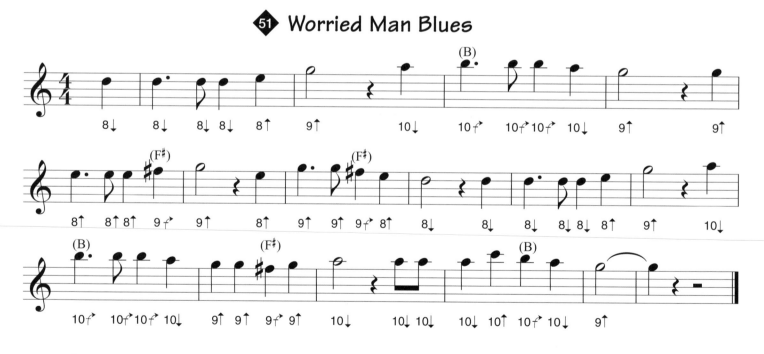

 WHY BOTHER?
You'll encounter lots of sharps and flats in all types of music,
especially the blues. Without bending,
you'd have to learn the chromatic harmonica to play these notes!

LESSON 6
Make the pros jealous!

Playing the notes well is half the battle. The other half is playing the notes with style. This lesson will probably be the most fun, and you can apply these tricks of the trade to any of the songs you play.

Vibrato

If you want to sound like the pros, one simple technique called **vibrato** can do the trick. Vibrato sounds like you're "wobbling" the note. Listen to Track 52 to hear an example. You'll hear the music first without vibrato, then again with vibrato.

Sounds great, huh? You can achieve this several ways. The easiest vibrato is called **hand vibrato**. (We have no idea why—maybe because you use your hand?!) Here's how it works:

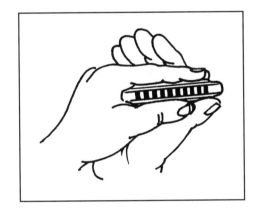 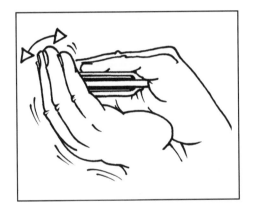

As you play a longer note—a half note or whole note—simply **flap the fingers** of your outside hand away from the harmonica and back, sort of like the flap of a bird's wing. (Make sure the palm of your hand does not move. It should stay cupped and in contact with your other hand.)

Try adding vibrato to each of the notes in this "scaly" exercise:

53 By the Wobbly C

The faster you "flap," the faster the vibrato. Try it again with various speeds of vibrato—first slow, then fast, then a mixture. Which do you prefer?

A nice effect that you can add virtually anywhere is the **slide**. All you do is start on a lower part of the harp and "slide" into the desired melody note or chord. Listen to some examples on Track 54.

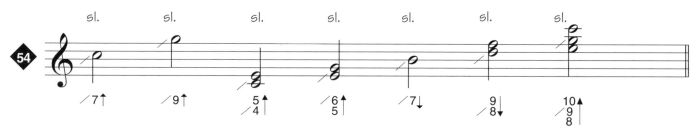

Play Track 54 again and try it yourself. Simply put your mouth on the starting note and keep blowing (or drawing) up to the next note. Once you get the hang of it, try it in a song.

NOTE: Don't forget to add some hand vibrato to the longer notes. These are marked with an **H.V.** (Well, what did you think "H.V." meant, silly?)

55 Battle Hymn of the Republic

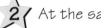 **Train whistle**

Here's a cool technique to apply to chords. The **train whistle** is a signature harmonica sound. (Well, OK, it's also a signature locomotive sound!) And it doesn't really matter if the chord sounds great—just make it sound cool.

Follow these easy steps:

 1 Draw Holes 4 and 5 together.

2 At the same time, say "WHA, WHAAA."

3 Also at the same time, wave your right hand in front of the open side of the harmonica.

Try it with this rhythm...

◆56 Train Whistle #1

In the previous lesson, you learned to bend single notes. You can bend chords, too! And when you do, you get another type of train sound:

 1 Draw Holes 1 and 2 (down low) together. (You can add Hole 3, too, if you like.)

2 Apply lots of pressure to bend these notes down and back up

3 At the same time, add some good ol' hand vibrato.

Signal your new train's station approach with a rhythm like this...

◆57 Train Whistle #2

PLAYING WITH TRAINS
Sure, it sounds cool. But how can you use it in a song?
Just about anywhere you think it sounds good. It's up to you!

LESSON 7
Some minor adjustments

Playing straight harp (key of C) and cross harp (G blues) are very popular ways to use your harmonica. Our last type of key has a name that sounds unimportant—**minor**—but don't be fooled. It's just a name. Minor keys are just as important as major and blues keys.

Key of A minor

Remember how powerful the F note was when played in a G blues song? Minor keys have their own power-wielding notes, causing minor keys to sound sort of "sad." Compare the first five notes of a C major scale compared to an A minor scale...

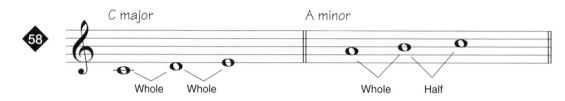

The reason they sound different (besides which root note they start on) is due to the step between the second and third note. In a major scale, this is a whole step. In a minor scale, this is a half step.

The key of **A minor** is well suited to your C diatonic harp, because it uses the exact same notes as C major—that is, no sharps or flats:

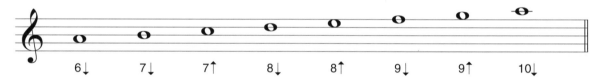

☞ NOTE: The best place to play A minor tunes is between Holes 6 and 10. But all of these notes (except lo A) are also on Holes 3 to 6.

The most common notes in this key are A, C, and E. Why? These notes make an **A minor chord.** Jam along with Track 59, playing As, Cs, and Es (or the riff we've written) to see how easy it is to improvise in A minor. Don't forget to throw in other scale notes for added flavor...

59 A Minor Riffs

40

You can hear the key of A minor at work in a well-known tune. Again, no new notes, but a completely different sound!

◆60 When Johnny Comes Marching Home

| 5↑ | 5↑ | 6↓ | 6↓ | 6↓ | 7↓ | 7↑ | 7↓ | 7↑ | 6↓ | 6↑ |

| 5↑ | 6↑ | 5↑ | 5↑ | 6↓ | 6↓ | 6↓ | 7↓ | 7↑ | 7↓ |

| 7↑ | 8↓ | 8↑ | 7↑ | 8↑ | 7↑ | 8↓ | 8↑ | 8↑ | 8↑ | 8↓ | 7↑ |

| 8↓ | 8↓ | 8↓ | 7↓ | 7↑ | 7↑ | 7↑ | 7↓ | 6↓ | 7↓ | 7↓ | 7↓ | 7↑ | 8↓ |

| 8↑ | 8↓ | 7↑ | 7↓ | 5↑ | 6↓ | 6↓ | 6↓ | 6↑ | 6↓ |

Key of E minor

The most common chord in the key of **E minor** is (you guessed it!) an **E minor chord**, which contains the notes E, G, B. So, if you're jamming along in E minor, make sure you throw these notes in.

☞ NOTE: If you just put your mouth around Holes 2 and 3, no matter what you play (blow or draw notes) will sound like E minor, since the only notes there are E, G, and B. Also, Holes 5 through 8 are good for songs in the key of E minor, since all the notes (from E to E) are there.

Try playing along with Track 61, emphasizing Es, Gs, and Bs. Then make your riffs more interesting with some other notes. One little tip, though—avoid the note F (we'll explain on the next page)...

◆61 E Minor Riffs

| 2↑ | 2↑ | 2↑ | 3↑ | 4↓ | 3↑ | 2↑ |

| 5↑ | 5↑ | 6↑ | 6↓ | 6↑ | 5↑ | 4↓ | 4↓ | 4↓ | 5↑ |

Just like the key of G, the key of E minor (technically) requires an F-sharp. But you don't have to play the F-sharp—just avoid it. You'll find songs in E minor (like the next one) that don't even use the F-sharp.

62 St. James Infirmary

Key of D minor

Last, but not least, the key of **D minor** is also a fun one because you can play a **D minor chord**! Notice that the notes of this chord—D, F, A—are located together on Holes 4 to 6 and Holes 8 to 10.

Blow	C	E	G	C	E	G	C	E	G	C
Hole	1	2	3	4	5	6	7	8	9	10
Draw	D	G	B	D	F	A	B	D	F	A

You can use these notes one at a time in a riff...

63 D Minor Riff

Or use the entire chord to jam with the band...

64 D Minor Chords

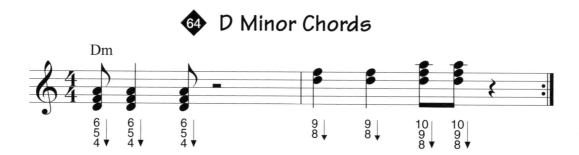

Technically speaking, the key of D minor requires a B-flat. But hey, plenty of D minor songs don't even use that note. In fact, the next D minor song actually uses a plain old B! (Go figure.)

65 Scarborough Fair

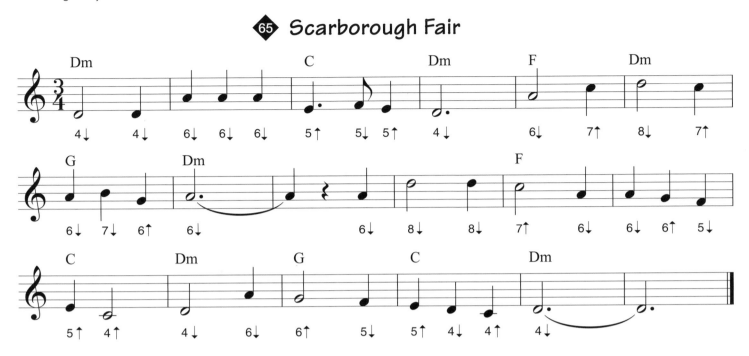

Since you know how to play the D minor chord, try "Scarborough Fair" again, but play the chords only. That's right—relax and let someone else play the melody for a while.

Minor chord options

You enjoy playing the D minor chord and want to play more minor chords? Good luck! A minor and E minor chords contain both blown and drawn notes. So, it's not possible to play all of the notes (at once) of these minor chords. Instead, you have some options...

Play the notes of the chord one at a time...   or use the two-note chord option from Lesson 4...

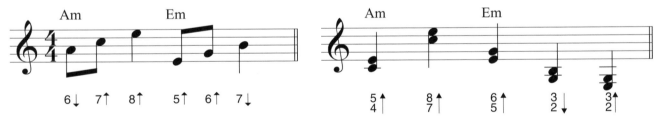

Either way (or both), you'll be able to riff your way out of any minor jam... no pun intended!

66 All Kinds of Minor Jam

* The slash marks mean to play the chord for those beats.

Time for quick phone break!
Call some friends and have them learn other
FastTrack™ instruments, so you can form a band.

LESSON 8

Time to charge admission...

This isn't really a lesson...it's a jam session!

All of the **FastTrack**™ books (harmonica, guitar, keyboard, bass, and drums) have the same last section. This way, you can either play by yourself along with the audio or form a band with your friends.

So, whether the band's on the audio or in your garage, let the show begin...

67 68 Exit for Freedom

full band | minus harmonica

Unplugged Ballad

GOOD THINGS TO KNOW

Before you move on to other musical endeavors, there are a few more things you should understand about harmonica playing. These tips will help you play virtually any music, in any key, with anyone.

Know the key

When you play music with others, it's very important to ask what key a song is in. If it's not in the key of C, and you don't feel that you can comfortably handle all of the sharps and flats on your C harp, then your solution is to use a **different key** diatonic harmonica.

Harmonicas are made in various keys (all keys, actually!). As you know, yours is in the key of C. But if you play the exact same music on a harmonica in A, all that changes is that the notes will sound lower. This is called **transposition**.

So, if you play this on an A diatonic harp...   the same music will sound like this...

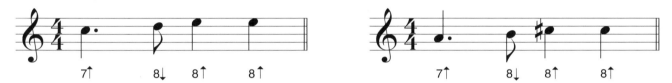

So, if the band says, "Let's try that song again in G," don't panic—just pull out your G harmonica and play the song again. You just instantly transposed!

Which do I buy?

You don't need to buy a harmonica for every single musical key, though. (In fact, you may only need the one you have.) If you are shopping for a new diatonic harmonica, here are the most common keys for various styles of music:

Style	Key	Harmonica
Rock	E, A, G, C	E, A, G, C
Blues	G, A, E, B-flat	C, D, A, E-flat
Pop	C, G, F, D, A	C, G, F, D, A
Folk	C, D, G, A	C, D, G, A

Where to go from here?

Here are some suggestions to help you continue to master the harmonica:

 Repetition is the best way to learn. Review the exercises in this book again and again until all the notes are easily playable without even thinking about them.

Buy *FastTrack™ Harmonica Songbook*, which includes great songs from some of your favorite artists.

 Enjoy what you do. Whether it's practicing, playing, jamming, or even stuffing your harmonica in your hip pocket, do it with a smile on your face. Life's too short.

See you next time...

SONG INDEX
(...what book would be complete without one?)